IN THE WORLD Alone

MY STORY

WENDY CRAIG

WITH THE ASSISTANCE OF DORIN HART

Nenge Books, Australia

In the World Alone - My Story
by Wendy Craig

Published by Nenge Books, Australia
ABN 26809396184
nengebooks1@gmail.com
www.nengebooks.com

Copyright © Wendy Craig 2019

First Published - July 2019
First revision - November 2019

This book or parts thereof may not be reproduced in any form, stored in a retrieval system or transmitted in any form without prior permission from the publisher.

Photographs - copyright © Wendy Craig 2019 except
Photo on page 41 copyright © FCNSW, used by permission.
Cover: original artwork by Wendy Craig - copyright © Wendy Craig 2019.
Design, desktop, editing and publishing by Nenge Books.

Nenge Books, a small business on the Mid-North Coast of NSW, specialises in publlishing smaller quantity runs of quality books using cost effective print-on-demand technology, and we comes enquiries to assist in publishing biographies and personal interest stories, as we l as other book publishing requests.

This book is available to order direct from the publisher (at nengebooks1@gmail.com) or from bookshops around the world.

ISBN 978-0-6484284-4-2

I would like to dedicate this book
to Ken and Marie for making
me a stronger person.

CONTENTS

The Turtle Painting	6
Forward	7
Introduction	9
My Story	11
Dalmar	13
Life at Dalmar - Childhood Memories	18
My family finds me	28
Westwood	34
21 at last	38
Rydalmere	39
A life of my own	42
My life now	44

THE TURTLE PAINTING

To me this painting (on the book cover) reminds me of my mother, siblings and childhood. My mother was a very strong woman who taught us how to be strong and to be there for one another as we were growing up.

I started painting in 1984. Although my disability can limit my capability in life, it has never stopped me doing what I love and that is painting.

Therefore this painting represents a mother leading her babies in Gumbaynggirr country at the jetty foreshores, guiding them through life, telling stories of the sea, land and the spirits of the dreamtime.

FORWARD

Little did I know when I agreed to assist Aunty Wendy with editing her story with a view to publishing it that it would be both the journey of a lifetime for her and be such an important addition to the documentation of Aboriginal children's lives.

Her story is one of survival. Acutely sick as a very small child and brought up in children's homes in Sydney, she always thought she was an only child and had no idea she was Aboriginal. Until one day in her teens everything changed.

Wendy's account of those times and her great achievement, after many years, being with her family in Coffs Harbour, makes "In the World Alone - My Story" also a story of success. And a dream come true.

For that has been Wendy's dream – to create a book of her story.

Congratulations, Wendy.

Dorin Hart - Writer

July 2019

CRAIG family tree

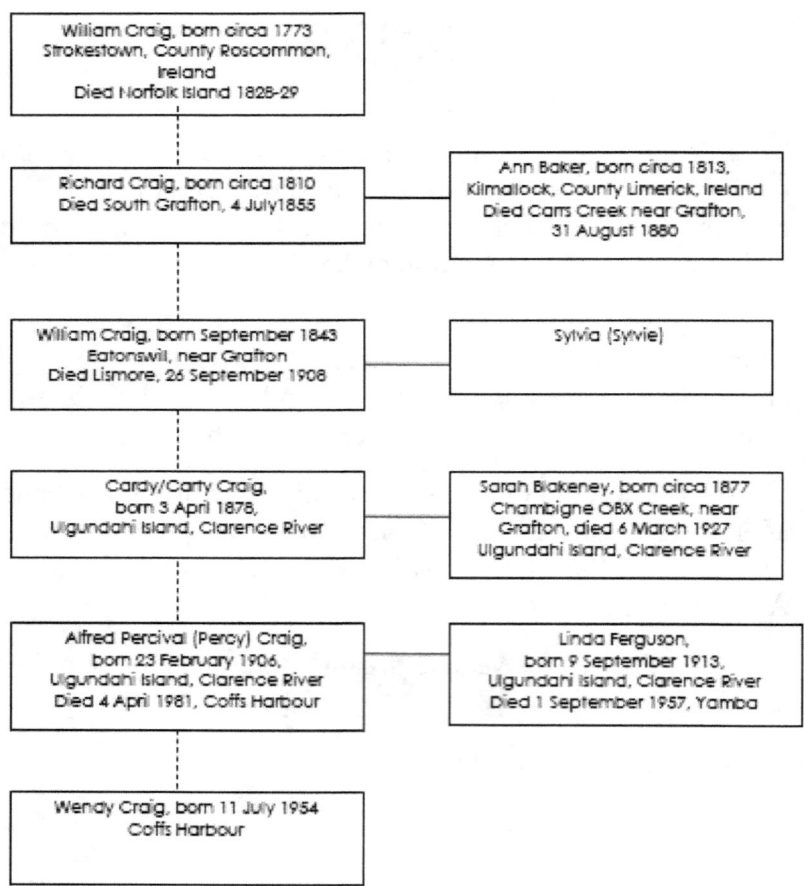

Sources:

1. *A Guide Record of Births Deaths and Marriages records from the private diary of Mr A E Cameron*, manager of Ulgundahi Island near Maclean, New South Wales
2. *Breimba Lindt Documents*, Folder 1, Family Trees A-K, Annika Korsgaard, 2014
3. NSW Registry of Births, Deaths and Marriages, https://bdm.nsw.gov.au
4. Records and Archives NSW, https://records.nsw.gov.au
5. Trove, https://trove.nla.gov.au
6. *North Coast Women, a history to 1939* by Baiba Berzins, 1996

Item 1 is held by the Maclean Museum
Item 2 is held by the Clarence Regional Library in Grafton, Local Studies section

INTRODUCTION

My name is Wendy Jane Craig. I am an Aboriginal woman from the Gumbaynggirr region which covers a great distance from Grafton to beyond Nambucca along the coast and inland in the Nymboida area of the NSW mid-north coast.

I was born on the 11th July 1954 in Coffs Harbour. My father was Percival Alfred Craig and my mother Linda Dianne Craig (nee Ferguson).

Wendy's parents, Percival Craig and Linda Fergusen marry - 12 November 1932 in Maclean, NSW.

I grew up in a children's home in Sydney thinking I was an only child. I had a general idea that my mum was dead but that my father was alive, though I didn't know where he was. I had no idea I was Aboriginal. I grew up in the whiteman's world in those days.

One day, when I was about fourteen, Matron rang the cottage that I was in.

"You have a visitor," she said.

"A visitor? But no one knows I'm here."

"Just come on over," said Matron.

A dark girl, a bit taller than me, and with wavy hair, was standing in the office.

"Wendy," Matron pointed to the girl, "This is your sister Linda."

"She's not my sister," I told Matron. "All I know is that I had a mother and a father." I must have carried on something dreadful. But it was true. Linda was my sister and after all these years she had come to find me.

It would be many more years before I met all my family and even longer before I lived once again in Coffs Harbour. Even though now I'd met my sister Linda and she said she would visit, I still felt I was in the world alone.

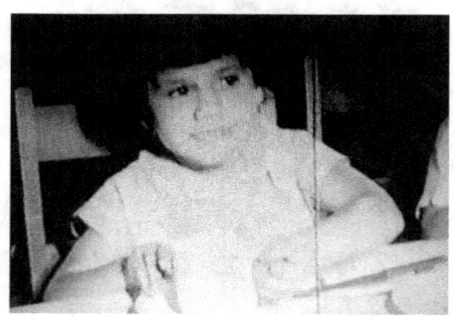

MY STORY

Linda told me that my mum had eleven children and that I had eight brothers and sisters still alive. We were all Aboriginal. Eldest to youngest, there was Kenneth Henry, Marie June, Arthur Percival, Sarah Elizabeth and Samuel John. Next was Linda Dianne then Fay Irene, then John Alexander who died young. Finally, there was me, Wendy Jane, my twin Brenda who also died young, and a younger brother, Lindsay Barry.

I just couldn't take it all in. And there was more. I had a twin, Brenda Kay who died when we were three months old. How I would have loved to have known her.

Now, years later, as well as my own memories I have stories from my family and old records I've searched. And this is what happened.

Lindsay was still a baby, not much more than a year old, and I was about three years old when my mother died. My big sister, Marie, stayed with Dad and looked after my baby brother and all the boys.

My sisters Sarah, Linda and Fay were put into Rathgar, a girl's home in South Grafton, but I was sent to Sydney. A lady by the name of Mrs Trustum, the Far West Children's Home Welfare Officer in Coffs Harbour, took me to the Far West Children's Home in Manly. I had polio and also convulsions as a baby and Mum and my sister Marie used to take me on the train to Sydney for treatment. I always stayed at the Far West Children's Home so this was where they sent me when Mum died.

My twin sister, Brenda, also had polio much worse than me. People in our family say that if Brenda had lived she would have been in a wheelchair for the rest of her life.

I was 18 months old when I went to stay at the Far West Children's home for about six months. Years later I got copies of all the letters the staff had written to my parents over that time, saying how I was improving, having treatment at the Mosman Spastic Centre. They sent letters every two weeks. They always said I was a bright cheery little girl. I don't remember anything much from those days but I do have happy memories of playing on the beach with the other kids.

When I was three and a half I was moved from the Far West Children's Home to Dalmar Children's home in Carlingford, Sydney. Dalmar was run by the Wesley Mission. They thought I would need to be in care there because of my polio and epilepsy. I was made a ward of state and lived at Dalmar until I was fifteen years old. Until I was fourteen, I had no contact with my family and thought I was an only child.

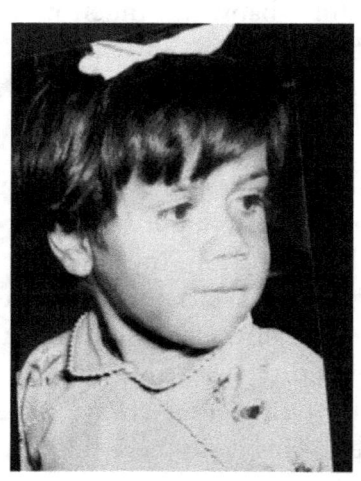

Wendy, three years old, at Dalmar

DALMAR

Dalmar was a big old house on a large property, like a small farm. It grew a lot of its own food. I have a copy of a film made about the home in 1958. It shows how the whole place was set up, with older children working in the gardens and milking the cows and driving the tractor. That film shows me twice, sitting with the others at mealtime. I was four and drinking a cup of milk. When I was older I also milked the cows.

There were up to a hundred children at Dalmar in those days. Most lived in big dormitories at the back of the main building, but I lived in Vickery, one of two newer cottages, with about ten other children.

Dalmar Childrens Home

17th September 1957

Mr. P. Craig,

KORORA WEST. NSW

Dear Mr. Craig,

    Wendy is keeping very well and has been fitted with her new boots and irons and is walking around very well in them. She was also seen by a physician who is quite pleased with her progress.

    We were very sorry to hear of your bereavement and we suppose you are finding it very difficult looking after the children. Have you someone to do this for you or are you trying to manage yourself, it is so sad when a mother is taken away from her little ones and we do hope you are not finding it too difficult

With love from Wendy.

Yours sincerely,

(Mrs.)

General Secretary & Matron

Text of one of the fortnightly letters sent by the Far West Children's Home, Manly, to Wendy's father outlining her progress.

AUNTY SHIRLEY

Aunty Shirley Smith was our house mother at Vickery Cottage. She was very kind, a caring person and looked after us well. She looked after the babies and right through until we left. After she left Dalmar she still kept contact, sending us Christmas cards. I still have contact with her today.

Aunty Shirley remembers me going to Vickery. She would always tell me, "You had to wear special boots. They put an iron boot and bands on one leg because you had polio when you were very young. Every so often I had to take you to the Spastic Centre over in Mosman for treatment."

There was a lot of treatment done to my right leg, it had to be stretched because it was two inches off the ground. It was very painful when they stretched it. It did grow gradually, but was never as long as the other.

Ready to go for a swim - Wendy is the third child up the steps.

My arm was also checked; it was very weak, still is today and I can't feel anything with it. I had all sorts of exercises to do for my leg, arm and especially my hand.

Aunty Shirley told me that as well as polio I also had seizures. I can remember when I was four years old I was sitting in the dining room having my lunch, it was a hot potato. I got dizzy and they had to put me in a cold bath, filled right up to the top, to get my temperature down.

"I remember the first time I saw you take an epileptic turn," Aunty Shirley said, "Matron Barnett had told me what to do. I always carried a peg with me to put in between your teeth and I would turn you on your side. That was what was done in those days. I still did panic although I tried not to show it but I was glad when Matron arrived at Vickery Cottage."

"Wendy, you and I accepted it in those days," Aunty Shirley said. "One time in church you had a turn and Jim Stewart, the

At the pool - Wendy is third from the back

Wendy at 7 yrs old

Superintendent of Dalmar, drove us back to the Home. Another time I had taken you and some other girls to Manly and just before we got onto the ferry to come back you had a turn. Thankfully the tablets you took helped a lot so the epilepsy became less and less."

By the time I was in my teens the seizures stopped completely.

Aunty Shirley reckoned I was very good at disappearing quickly when I was young and had my favourite places. "It seemed you were always to be found in the square near the back door of the kitchen where the bins were kept and you would come back with something out of the bin that wasn't any good anymore," she said.

"You seemed to me to get on well with the other girls in the cottage but I believe you did use your boot with the iron caliper on it for kicking when a disagreement happened." Later old Dalmar friends I have met at our reunions have agreed with this!

Aunty Shirley also told me, "Although you had disabilities with your arm and legs you never complained and it did not stop you from trying to do things. You always had a big smile and a hearty laugh and could talk to everybody and anyone you liked. You were never shy."

LIFE AT DALMAR – CHILDHOOD MEMORIES

I can remember when I was very young walking from the cottage to go up to the Dalmar kindergarten every day. Then I went to Carlingford Primary. After a while I was sent to Northcott Crippled Children's School, Parramatta. I got help there using my leg, also my arm and hand, like how to tie up my shoelaces. At first I went by taxi, then the bus.

Aunty Shirley always told me, "I would look before you left Vickery and waited at the front of Dalmar for the taxi. Sometimes Matron looked to make sure you had not packed something you shouldn't have. I still don't know how you managed to get the things in your school bag you shouldn't have had." I have no idea nowadays what these things were. They were always very strict with us.

I remember going on the bus by myself and having an accident. One day, just after my tenth birthday, I fell off the bus. I thought it was not going to stop, so I just jumped off at my stop. I know the bus driver was very upset and came to the hospital to see me. Years later, when I got back some of my records, I found this official report from the Dalmar superintendent to the Child Welfare Department:

> She apparently alighted from the bus while it was still in motion and fell heavily to the ground puncturing her forehead and grazing her knee and elbow, she was brought home unconscious, by a passing motorist. Wendy was then taken to Ryde Hospital where her wounds were dressed and an appointment was made for an X-ray.

When I was eleven and a half I started at Hassall Street, Parramatta, another special school for children with mild disabilities. By then my legs were out of irons and I was apparently progressing well, with no after effects from the bus accident. I was taken to this school by car.

Every year when our birthday came we would get thrown into the pool, in the deep end. Because my birthday was in the winter time I was thrown in with my clothes on. Depending on how old you were turning, that was the amount of times you were thrown into the pool by the other kids.

Wendy riding on shoulders

I could swim, but it was scary being thrown in. I wished my birthday was in summer. That would have been more fun.

We had an old blue tram at Dalmar at the back of the cottage that I was in. I remember when I was about ten we would play in the tram and sometimes sleep there. The cows would come right up to the tram in the night and make a noise so we could not go back to sleep. When we got up the next day we would have some breakfast and go to school. I remember one time jumping off the top of the tram and hurting my ankle. I had to go and get it bandaged up.

When I was about four an older lady, her husband and two daughters saw me playing on the monkey bar at Dalmar. I remember one girl came up and asked my name.

"Wendy," I replied. She was Joyce and her sister was Val. That family took me as a foster child to their place for holidays. Joyce would also come to see me all the time, even after I was moved to another home. When she got married she would come with her husband, Bob Heslop. I still keep in touch with her today.

Every year in November we had a fete at the Children's Home and we would get dressed up. One year I was a marching girl, a Christmas bon-bon the next year and a clown the following year, it was lots of fun.

We had fun too at the Channel 7 TV studios. I can remember going up from Dalmar every Saturday morning to the studios up on top of the hill in Epping. In those days it was just a walk up from Carlingford for us through the bush. We were part of the audience for the Uncle Reggie show, a children's entertainment program.

Then people came sometimes to Dalmar to film us kids for TV advertisements they showed on Channel 9 and Channel 10. We were in Coca Cola ads, one for Weetbix and then one for Smarties with the 'Buy some for Lulu' jingle. That one was great. We were all dressed up as Red Indians, I had a plait and headband of feathers. In the ad we had to throw boxes and boxes of Smarties all around the place.

Every month a group of people from Wiley Park Church would come to the Home to play games with us, like spin the bottle. One time we had a bonfire night with them. They always made a special fuss of me because of my leg.

There were times when we would do naughty things. Every time we walked up the hill to go to the local school we would eat a buttercup flower. We would pull the green stem off the yellow flower and eat the stem. If we got caught eating this flower we would get a dose of castor oil when we got home. I did it because it was lots of fun and I wanted to. Sometimes you didn't get caught by the staff because they were down the bottom of the hill.

Wendy on John's shoulders

I do remember putting a piece of paper in the fire and a piece of hot plastic wrapped around my thumb and I had to go to the Matron so she could bandage it up and I had to stay home for the rest of the day.

We all got on well together, the different ages. I don't know why, but the bigger ones all liked me and gave me piggyback rides all around the yard. I especially remember one, John Laws, carrying me on his back down the driveway. I have a photo of that. I can also remember drawing on boxes, decorating them, with another girl.

The staff were pretty strict with us at Dalmar. We often got hit on our hands with the cane. If you did something really bad you could get the strap. That was given by the Superintendent, Donald Stewart, he was in charge of the whole home.

Chalk drawing, Wendy on right.

I remember getting into things that got me in trouble, like going into the Matron's bedroom and putting makeup on or into the office and finding things I would put in my bag and take to school.

Most of the time I kept out of trouble, but I did do a few wild things. One time the tractor was parked outside the front door with the key in it. I climbed on and started it up. Matron heard it. She came out straight away and told me to get off it. I got punished for that - I can't remember though whether I got the strap or just the cane!

When I was 11 years old I didn't have to wear the special

boot and irons on my leg any more. Matron Dorothy Barnett said to me, "Wendy, I have got some shoes for you to try on." They were black buckle up shoes, so special, the very first pair of smart shoes I'd ever had. I would wear them to Sunday School.

Some of Wendy's brothers and sisters, L to R: Sam, Arthur, Linda, Marie holding baby Barry.

Aunty Bessie, Wendy's mother's sister.

Remembering our experiences with Wendy – notes from family and former residents of the Children's Home:

Debbie: "I remember when Wendy and Debbie found some money and we ran off to the shops and bought some lollies. We ate them all and on return we got busted."

Kathy: "I remember helping Wendy with her exercises to strengthen her leg. She would have something tied to her leg that she would have to lift up and down. I used to tell her to hurry up so we could go and play.

Another time Wendy found a key to Shirley's room. She moved a cupboard away from one door. Wendy, Jenny, Kathy and Debbie went into the room and had a sticky beak in the cupboards. Then we got out of there because we were scared that we'd get caught.

Arthur, the brother of Jenny, Kathy and Debbie, liked Wendy. Arthur used to like playing marbles. Wendy was excellent at marbles. She used to win lots of the big marbles. We all had our own collection of marbles in our own locker.

Shirley let us all sleep in the side of the tram. We made a cubby house there with sheets to make places to hide. Shirley would come out and wait at the door because she knew we would come back in if we heard a noise. We came in screaming because we thought people were around. It turned out it was just the cows in the next paddock.

We had a pogo stick and stilts and a penny farthing bike and we were always fighting over them. We used to get the jigsaw puzzles out when it is was raining.

We used to play hopscotch a lot. Wendy used to try her hardest because she had a brace on her right leg.

We used to have bonfire nights with people from Wiley Park Methodist church. The boys used to throw crackers at the cows and put the crackers in the cow manure and watch the explosion! Debbie said something like a burning cinder got in Wendy's eye from the fire, so they decided bonfire nights were too dangerous to have anymore."

Jenny: "We walked up to Channel Seven and got into mischief. We'd sneak into some of the shows.

We used to go down to the creek and bring the tadpoles back and put them in the laundry sink. Shirley would go in there the next morning and they would have turned into frogs.

We used to play on the swings and Debbie got her teeth broken with the swing.

One of the workers used to throw us kids into the swimming pool when we had a birthday,

We helped the boys build a cubby house up in a tree in the paddock. But it burned down!

Wendy didn't like peas. We used to get a pen and flick them at the boys and the rice.

We used to have the plays and we used to dress up for the fun of it.

We used to go to Girl Guides at Pennant Hills.

We had a lot of celebrities come to the home even some circus people. Every Saturday night we watched movies on the big screen up in the main building.

The boys used to milk the cows but when they had a holiday the girls had to try to milk them."

"Having known Wendy since 1960 during the time at Vickery Cottage and being an older girl, I used to give therapy to her right leg in the form of stretching exercises before her caliper was then put back on her leg. This was done once daily.

Being an older girl, I assisted with showering and dressing of Wendy and organising daily chores. I remember her as an eager young girl, who was well behaved."

Judy Tyler, November 2017

"When we all got together, Wendy would chase us with sticks because we made her angry."

Terry Wickey, December 2017

"Wendy was teased by the other kids because she had polio as a child. Terry and I used to stand up for her and protect her."

Julie Maggs, December 2017

Wendy (with dark hair) in the playground

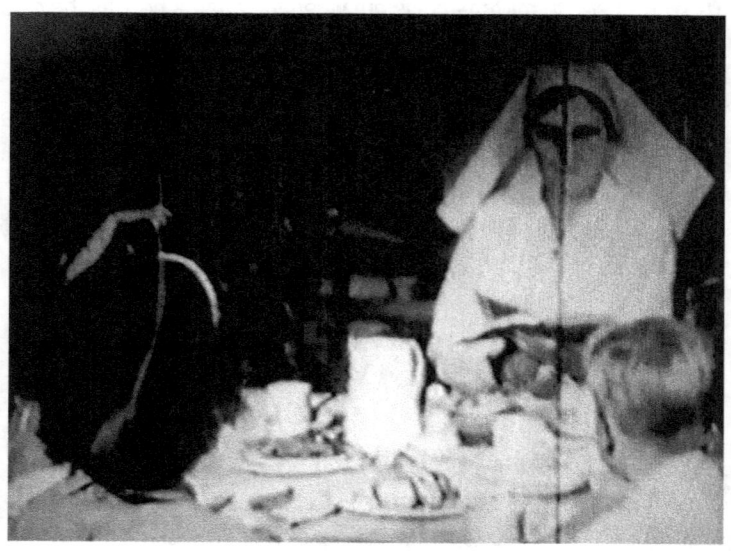

"Wendy was 4 years old and had been taken to Dalmar Children's Home at Carlingford, as her father was unable to look after all his children when their mother had died. The children were sent to different places (about which I have no knowledge) but in later years her sister was able to reunite them.

At the time my sister Val was overseas and I was lonely, so it was suggested we ring Dalmar, which my Dad and I did. Dalmar said they had a little girl there who was 4 and who would like to stay for weekends. Perhaps later when she had started kindergarten and school, she could stay in the school holidays. Wendy was disabled through polio, which had affected her arm and leg and when she was young she needed quite a lot of extra care.

My father and I used to drive over to Dalmar at Carlingford and pick her up, which she enjoyed. The other little girls and boys were also happy to see us.

Wendy used to call my parents Mum and Dad, and even now at 64 she keeps in touch with my family.

When Wendy was about 6, I married Bob and he was happy to go over to Dalmar and pick her up, like my father did. We used to take her out to the beach, the park and other places to play when she had a great time. Sometimes neighbour's children would come with us. We also visited my family. Wendy came to church and Sunday School when she stayed with us.

Dalmar remains in contact with Wendy, sending her invitations to her reunions.

When Wendy was older she moved to a different estabishmemt at Bowral, from where we continued to pick her up."

Joyce Heslop, 21 October 2017

MY FAMILY FINDS ME

All this time I did not know that I had four brothers and four sisters that my Mother had eleven children all together. I did not know that I was a twin, or that one brother, John A Craig, the next oldest to me, had also died. My sister Marie, who later was like my mum when I came to meet my family, told me about him and where he is buried.

On that day when Matron called me to her office and said 'Wendy, this is your sister, Linda,' my life turned around.

At first I said over and over again, "She's not my sister. I just have a mum and a dad!" I must have carried on something dreadful. I remember I made Linda cry and I ended up crying myself.

There was another, older lady in Matron's office, this was Linda's landlady. It was she who finally made me understand that Linda really was my sister.

Linda was living in Sydney and working in a hospital in the city. Linda told her landlady that she had a sister somewhere in a children's home, but she didn't know how to find me. This lady helped Linda find me by ringing round all the church homes in the city around the Missions in Sydney. Finally, she rang Dalmar Children's Homes and they said they had a Wendy Craig there. Without that lady, Linda would never have found me.

Linda spent the whole day with me on that first visit. She told me that my eldest brother, Ken, was 34, sister Marie, 24. Then Arthur was 21, Sarah, 20 and Sam 18. Linda herself was

17 and Fay 15. Barry, 'the baby', was now 12. I just couldn't take it all in.

Afterwards my friends asked who my visitor was. I still wasn't sure about it all. "I think she is my sister," I remember saying.

I had no idea I was Aboriginal; neither did any of my friends. They were surprised. They just thought I had olive skin. There was just one family of Aboriginal children at Dalmar.

Wendy at 13 yrs old

Well Linda came to see me every weekend. One time she asked me whether I would like to go with her to the pictures and take a friend too. We saw 'The Sound of Music'. This was the first time I had been to the pictures. Another time Linda brought her fiancé.

Then one weekend she came to visit with a different man. This was my brother Sam, next oldest after Linda, come to visit from Coffs Harbour. Sam took me out to a Koala Park at Pennant Hills for a day trip. When I was there I was eating a packet of chips and an emu came up behind me and was pecking at my packet of chips so I had to give it my chips.

When the May holidays came another of my sisters, Fay came to stay at Dalmar for the holidays. This was the first time I had met her. She was living at Rathgar Children's Home in Grafton where all my sisters had been sent after Mum died. She and I went into the city to a park and she climbed a tree and she carved her name with her boyfriend's name.

We went for a walk around the big city, Sydney, then we got the train back to the Dalmar at Carlingford. Fay stayed there until it was time to say goodbye. When she went back to Coffs Harbour she told everyone about me and that she had another sister and that I was in a Children's Home.

When the August holidays came and I was fifteen I got a telegram at Dalmar saying I could go for a holiday at Rathgar.

Wendy meets her family in Coffs Harbour, 1969:
(Back) Dad, Ken, Marie, (front) Fay, Wendy & Linda

But instead of Grafton, I got off the train at Coffs Harbour and went to stay with my family.

That first time Aunty Shirley took me on the train- she was going on holidays to her parents in Lismore. Aunty Shirley said she remembered how excited I was to visit my family. It was exciting, but scary too.

My eldest brother Ken met me at the station and took me to stay with his family. I did not know Ken at all. He and his wife, Anita, had an older son, Reggie, the same age as me, then Rhonda, Ken Junior, and John and little ones, Mark and Randall. At first, though, I was scared to meet them all. In fact, I wouldn't get out of the car.

First we drove to my sister Marie's house, everyone else got out and went inside, but I stayed in the car. Ken tried to get me to go, but I just couldn't move. Fay tried also. Then finally Marie came and said, "Come on. Your dad's inside, d'you want to come and see him? He wants to meet you." So I hopped out of the car and ran inside to Dad and cried on his shoulder.

Dad was a very quiet man. I never got to know him well. Marie told me he was a gentle, well-mannered person. He never laid a hand on any of my brothers and sisters. I just saw him once on that holiday.

My sister Marie was living down at the railway line, which was at that time called Happy Valley and that is where I hurt my right big toe. I did not lift my right leg high enough and I grazed my toe on the barbwire fence. We would run down the hill where we lived and swing from a weeping willow tree and jump into the creek on the hot days. It was lots of fun. And there were sad things too.

Marie told me that I had a twin sister, Brenda Kay, who died when we were three months old. I had never known that. It made me sad to think that I never knew her and for many years after I'd shed a tear for her at our birthday and at Christmas.

Not all my family were still living around Coffs Harbour. Linda was in Sydney and Sarah was living on the south coast. At the end of the holiday I went back on the train to Sydney and Dalmar with Aunty Shirley.

Ken was very kind. Before I left we went to the service station at the promenade and he bought me all sorts of things for the train trip. Lollies and so on.

Proud Mums: Aunty Beryl holding son Artie, Aunty Bessy (Mum's sister), Wendy's Mum holding sister Marie, (front) Ally Boy (Aunty Bessie's son), cousing Desi (Uncle Lawrie, Mum's brother, Aunty Marg's son), Ken (Wendy's eldest brother).

WESTWOOD

When I turned fifteen in 1969 I was told I had to leave Dalmar and go to another home, Westwood Girls Home at Bowral. No one asked me if I wanted to go! And I just did not want to go.

A social worker took me to Westwood. We drove up the driveway which had flower beds on each side and I could see this big house and there was a tennis court in the front. As we came around the corner I could see another big house.

I arrived just on lunch time but I just felt like going upstairs to bed and crying my eyes out. There were four beds in each room. At first I was the only Aboriginal girl there but later two other girls came, Bronwyn Naiden, from Goulburn and Rosie Atkins from out west of Sydney.

Wendy (right) at Westwood

I felt strange and unhappy at the new home. There were about a hundred girls there and at first I only knew one girl. Her name was Lorna Mason and she worked in the laundry. She had been at Dalmar Home with me and she looked after me at Westwood.

I stayed at Westwood for nine years, until 1978. I did not like it at all. The staff in charge were called 'Sister', but they were not nurses and they were not always caring. It was not a nice place to stay; they always told us we could not get out of there. We would be told to do a lot of work.

All the girls had to do some work at Westwood. Some worked in the kitchen, some worked upstairs others worked in the dining room or the laundry, we all had something to do. Some girls did the cooking over in the other building, they made cakes and biscuits. One day I can remember walking downstairs to the kitchen to get a pot of tea. I missed a step on the way back up and fell over. The pot of tea scalded my legs so I had to get them bandaged up.

Westwood also had a sheltered workshop. I remember going there and doing lots of things like making bags, tablecloths and place mats with cross-stitch embroidery on them. We even put together toasters and heaters. It was hard work and tricky too; we worked for six hours a day five days a week. Other girls from around the area came there too. We Westwood girls got paid, but not much, and we didn't ever see it as it went to the home for our board money.

When I was seven-teen I can remember walking up and down the stairs at Westwood; I had pain on the left side on my stomach and then it went to my right side. I didn't know then, but it was appendicitis. I couldn't sleep that night. Sister Cooper said, "You're not sick," and made me get out of bed and go over and work in the sheltered workshop. When I got there one of the ladies said "You don't look well, Wendy," and I said, "I know." I told her that Sister Cooper had told me to come over to work. I went back to bed and stayed there until another sister came on the Wednesday.

That sister read the report and then came up to see me and said, "You're really sick."

"Yes I am," I replied.

She got one of the ladies to take me to hospital. When the doctor came and looked at me he said I had to have my appendix out. It was close to bursting, which would have been very dangerous. I stayed in hospital for a while after the operation. Westwood was far away from Sydney and Linda wasn't able to visit me there, though Aunty Joyce came sometimes.

One day when I was about seventeen, I was playing tennis on the tennis court when big Robyn came over and said to me, "You have a visitor."

"No I haven't," I said. "No one knows I'm here."

"Yes, you have. A lady wants to see you," she told me.

I dropped the tennis racquet and raced around the front. There was an Aboriginal woman standing in the office. I had never seen her before. One of the staff came up to me and said, "This is your sister."

I felt like saying once again, "No she's not." Although I had met some family in Coffs Harbour I didn't know where all of them lived and I still felt I was just in the world on my own.

This visitor turned out to be my older sister, Sarah, who I had never met until then. Linda had told her about me. Sarah lived in Wollongong and her husband had driven her over. Also in the car was a niece, Rhonda, and my Dad. They were down from Coffs Harbour, living with Sarah. I didn't recognise Dad at first as I had only met him briefly, on my one visit to Coffs.

After that I went to Sarah and her family in Wollongong for some holidays and Christmas. I also got to meet my brother Arthur who lived down that way. One time later Sarah came to visit me at Westwood but Sister said I had been mucking up - but I hadn't been, it was someone else who got me in to trouble

- so Sarah couldn't see me.

Then I got to work away from Westwood. One day, Sister came up to me and said. "Would you like to go and work at a coffee shop. It's down town, Bowral. They sell tea, coffee, sandwiches, cakes and biscuits." I said I would like it very much, so I worked there for a while. Later on another job came up at a canteen in a factory in Moss Vale. I was selling pies and other food. This was a very good job, but I never saw any of my wages; it all went to Westwood for board. We didn't even get any pocket money.

There were some good times at Westwood. Some girls, maybe they were students, came to the homes to play games with us, soft ball and so on. One of the girls was very interested to hear I came from Coffs Harbour, her home. Her name was Judy Small. Later I found out that this Judy Small became a famous singer.

In October and November, the gardens were full of tulips. We had a Tulip Time Fair. The day was a big fundraiser. All the goods we made at Westwood, table cloths, placemats and so on were on sale. Loads of buses came from Sydney, out west, even Melbourne, for the day. We were all dressed in Dutch costumes and served morning teas, lunches, afternoon teas. I remember carrying huge, heavy trays of food out to the tables for the visitors.

Westwood

21 AT LAST

When I was at Westwood Girls' Home I turned 21. I wanted to go home to Coffs Harbour for my birthday but the staff wouldn't let me. So I kicked up a stink and it worked. In the end the vicar, or maybe it was a priest, said to me, "You are going home for your birthday." I was so happy.

Before I went to Coffs Harbour my Aunty Shirley and Aunty Enid Kerr from Dalmar came to Westwood, and gave me a special cake for my 21st birthday.

In Coffs Harbour I stayed with my brother Sam and his wife Anne. My sister Linda came down too and I saw my Dad. He was staying at my other sister, Fay's house, and he gave me twenty dollars for my 21st Birthday. That was a lot of money in those days. We had a little party for my birthday.

I just wanted to stay in Coffs Harbour, but my family said I could not. No one ever explained why. Maybe it was because I was still on medication for epilepsy, though I didn't get seizures any more. I had to go back to Westwood.

I did not like going back to Westwood at all because the staff at that time were not very nice to the girls. I didn't get punished, but certain girls were all the time. There was one girl named Rose and she would get into trouble all the time. She would give cheek to the staff and when they told her off she would just give more cheek. A Sister would lock Rose in the staircase and she would keep her there without anything to eat. Then Rose would kick the door in and so she would be in trouble again. Trouble was her name!

RYDALMERE

One day in 1978, I would have been 24, someone came up to me at Westwood and told me I was to go to Rydalmere Psychiatric Hospital, not because I had mental problems. She said it was so that I could learn more living skills and it would be only for a while. Then I would be able to live outside in a group house with other people. I didn't like the idea of moving, but I had to go.

Rydalmere was a huge psychiatric hospital and there was no group house. I was in Ward 16 with about eleven other girls. I did not like that place at all. That was an open ward, you could come and go, but if they wanted, they could lock you in that place and not let you out at all. There were some wards, like Ward 12, where residents were locked in all the time.

I did make some friends, but on the whole I kept to myself. I didn't feel like talking to the others; some were mentally disturbed and a bit scary. Many were on heavy medication and some had the shakes. Some of the staff were okay but some were really nasty; they didn't talk to you properly. They talked as if there was something mentally wrong with you. It wasn't the right place for me.

The first skill to learn was cooking, but I didn't need to do that as I already knew how. Instead I had to teach six other girls to cook. That didn't work out. The kitchen was in a house where some of their boyfriends lived so half of those girls just wanted to muck about.

I ended up just staying at Rydalmere and going to work outside at the Parramatta Sheltered Workshop. In those days it was in town right next to the Parramatta Leagues Club. We made toasters and heaters again, just like when I was at Westwood. And we got paid properly. The wages were good and we were allowed to keep it all.

I always wanted to leave Rydalmere and would keep asking about that. They said it would be just on trial at first, for me to see what it was like to live out there. I said, seeing as I was working outside, I already knew what it was like. But they paid no attention. And no trial happened; I stayed on there for about three years. There were no activities at Rydalmere, no pool, like at Dalmar. We could go out occasionally, to the pictures. I would often go for walks on my own for something to do.

Sometimes my friend, Aunty Joyce, her husband Bob and their boys, would come to visit me there, but apart from that no one else came.

We did go as a group each year from Rydalmere for a few days holiday to Morriset. I remember we'd get there and put all our things down in the rooms, then we'd go down to the beach and go for a swim as well. Lunch would be in a park and we would go for walks. Then we'd go back on the bus and home to Sydney.

I was very lonely at Rydalmere. I don't know why I was kept there so long. Looking back on it now I wonder how I managed all those years there. But I did.

One day when I got paid at the Sheltered Workshop I didn't go back to Rydalmere. I had left some clothes at a friend's place, Kerry, out at Harris Park, and stayed there for a couple of weeks, but still went to work.

I rang up the Rydalmere office and told them I was alright, but they wanted to see me. So I went back with a friend. They tried to get me to go back but I refused and went back to the house I was staying at in North Parramatta. In the end a girl living with the others told the Rydalmere people I was mucking up. Actually I wasn't. But the Rydalmere people believed her and came to get me.

After that they locked me up in Ward 12 for a couple of weeks. Every door you went through on the way to Ward 12 was kept locked, five or six doors to unlock and lock, even when you went out into the courtyard. The people there, boys and girls, were really mentally ill. I wasn't. I was just put there for punishment for staying away. Eventually I got back into Ward 16 and went back to work.

But then one day I left work for good and never went back. Again it was pay day and I just took my pay and went. I stayed at Kerry's again. This time nobody came after me. I knew what I was doing, so they let me stay out. My life in homes and institutions was over.

A LIFE OF MY OWN

Some time after that I went on a holiday to all my family in Coffs Harbour and stayed with them for a while. Then my brother Ken and his wife Anita gave me an address in Sydney of their friend, Desi Fergusen. I could stay with him and his family out at St Mary's. When I told the taxi driver to take me to 117 Maple Street, he said "Oh that place. About twenty people live there!" But it wasn't like that at all. There weren't twenty people, just a big family, cousins of mine, and their friends and relatives who came and went.

When I asked a little boy on the doorstep to take me to Desi Fergusen he said, "I'm Desi Fergusen."

"No, I mean your father, Desi!" When I met his father and said, "I'm Wendy. Kenny and Anita said to say hello," he just looked and said, "Well, F... me dead! The last time I saw you, you were a baby!" I got there on a Sunday, just in time for lunch. It took them about two weeks to get used to me as an adult. I lived with them for a while.

Then I moved into the city, around Erskineville, Haberfield and back out west, Mount Druitt, Westmead, West Parramatta, all the time living in shared houses. I looked around for work but it was difficult to get jobs.

In April 1981 I was living out at Mt Druitt when this girl, Bonnie Wilson, came to see me and told me that my father had died, on 4th April. At first I could not believe what she told me. I went back to Coffs Harbour for his funeral. It was a very upsetting time for me. Standing at the graveside, I wished I could have gone down with him. I couldn't cope with anything for a while after that, but I didn't end up in hospital. I stayed a week or so then went back to Sydney.

Finally, I went back to Coffs Harbour and I gradually got to meet all the rest of my family and their friends. I got a job in Target and lived in Sawtell, on my own. Once I got out of the homes I always lived on my own. From that time on I could do anything, go anywhere without people telling me what to do.

Marie, my eldest sister became like a mum to me. She was thirteen when my mum died and told me all about Mum. Mum was a very small person, very pretty and quite light skinned. From birth she had one 'little' hand, not fully developed, but she could do all the work, everything - change nappies, do all the washing. With that little hand she could still punch out the damper dough; she made wonderful damper.

Mum's house was spotless. She would clean her house out then say to the kids, if they had been swimming and were dropping with water, "Don't you dirty the house now. I've just cleaned it!" Mum also couldn't hear at all; even so she managed to shop, do everything. One man in Coffs used to do sign language with her.

I went to Broken Hill for a holiday and stayed on for a while. I got into a relationship and had a baby there, William, in 1985. I lived there until I found the father was playing around on me. So I went back to Coffs Harbour and reared my son on my own. When I had to go back to Broken Hill for a court appearance, my sister Marie looked after William for me until I came back. I looked after William all by myself and did a very good job. In Coffs I got to meet more family and cousins I had not known before. I have a lot of family living in Coffs and talking to them over the years heard more of my family stories.

MY LIFE NOW

I'm no longer in the world alone. Coffs Harbour is my home; I've lived here ever since leaving those institutions. I brought up my son William here and I have friends and family nearby. I still have the shorter leg and weak arm and hand from polio but it doesn't stop me from getting out and about. I do need help around the place and nowadays William has come back to be my carer.

My great sadness in recent years is that first Ken and then Marie passed away. They have been the most important people in my life here; Marie was like my mother. I do so miss their support and all their knowledge about our people. Now I'm a Gumbaynggirr elder, like they were. I was so proud to do the Welcome to Country at the opening of the Department of Forestry's new lookout at Korora Bay. It has a memorial there to my brother, Ken, who worked with the department all his life

Over the years I've done many courses, often through TAFE, like baking, cake making and kitchen operations but the most important one was in 1994 discovering that I could do dot paintings in traditional Aboriginal style. I had never painted before then, never did art at school. Since then I've done many smaller paintings but also murals and I love doing banners for local Aboriginal events including the Aboriginal Elders Olympics, one of my favourite events of the year. I always take part and have helped organise them in Coffs Harbour. Aboriginal Elders Olympics covers from Moree, Tamworth and Dubbo to Port Macquarie and the Blue Mountains. Whoever wins the games hosts it the next year. It's real good fun, gets us elders out, visiting other communities, catching up with people. We even get on TV news.

I keep contact with the rest of my family as best I can. Fay, the closest in age, lives in my street; Sarah is nearby in Sawtell. Linda, who found me, lives in Green Pigeon, just out of Byron Bay, and Sam is at Woolgoolga. My other brothers, Arthur and Barry, live on the south coast. I have cousins, nieces and nephews as well. Some of my oldest cousins are in Maclean where Mum and Dad first lived and remember them clearly. I'm still collecting stories from that time.

Opening of Gumgali Track in Orara East State Forest. Aunty Wendy & Uncle Barry Hoskins, with MP's Luke Hartsuyker & Andrew Fraser and Dean Anderson, Forestry Corp. NSW.

Of course I have another family - the kids I grew up with at Dalmar. Not so many left now, but a few of us keep contact and Dalmar has regular get togethers for former residents. It's been very exciting to meet up there with a few from my time and swap stories. Aunty Shirley Smith, too old to travel now, is still alive and still remembers me. She always sends a Christmas card.

Now I have a new family, members of the stolen generation. I'm on the board of directors of Link Up, an Aboriginal organisation that helps people find their families.

I am so lucky to have met up with my own family I just want to help as many others to do the same.

The Honourable Don Harwin MLC
Leader of the Government in the Legislative Council
Special Minister of State
Minister for the Public Service and Employee Relations, Aboriginal Affairs, and the Arts
Vice-President of the Executive Council

Ms Wendy Craig
10 Kurrajong Street
Coffs Harbour NSW 2450

Dear Ms Craig

The Premier of NSW and the Prime Minister of Australia have apologised to Aboriginal people for the intentional removal of Aboriginal children from their parents, families, communities and culture. The laws and policies which enabled government representatives to remove children are recognised as causing Aboriginal people profound ongoing and intergenerational trauma.

I now apologise to you, on behalf of the State of New South Wales, for your removal from your father, Mr Percival Craig, and for the separation of you from your siblings. The State of New South Wales was responsible for your removal and placements in institutions following the loss of your mother while you were receiving treatment at the Far West Children's Home in Manly. You should never have been removed from your family and community.

I acknowledge that as a result of being removed, you were taken from your Gumbaynggirr homeland and denied your Aboriginal heritage. I am sorry that you did not get to grow up with your siblings or spend a childhood with your loving father. The institutions you were placed in could never replace the care and support of growing up in your family and community, and they did not provide you with the cultural nourishment.

It is clear your removal had a significant impact on you and your family. To your credit, despite this trauma you have gone on to reconnect with your family and culture, which shows great strength and resilience. It is a tribute to your happy and caring nature that others such as Aunty Shirley and the Heslop family were drawn to you. I would also like to acknowledge the important role of your sister Linda in connecting you to your family again, your sister Marie for becoming like a second mother, and your brother Ken for providing you with so much love and support.

Thank you for sharing your story. I appreciate that sharing it can be difficult as it may bring up painful memories. You have our deep gratitude as it is important for us to listen and learn from your experiences. I would also like to congratulate you on your book *In the World Alone, My Story*. It is an excellent book and I am sure it brings you great pride.

I hope this apology and recognition of the hurt that your removal caused assists you in some way, although I recognise that the memory of your experiences will remain with you always.

Yours sincerely

Don Harwin MLC
Minister for Aboriginal Affairs

21 OCT 2019

GPO Box 5341 Sydney NSW 2001 ▪ P: (02) 8574 7200 ▪ F: (02) 9339 5568 ▪ W: nsw.gov.au

www.ingramcontent.com/pod-product-compliance
Lightning Source LLC
Chambersburg PA
CBHW072115290426
44110CB00014B/1916